rare earth

rare earth
By Bradford Tice

Winner of the Many Voices Project

new
RIVERS
PRESS
MSUM

©2013 by Bradford Tice
First Edition
Library of Congress Control Number: 2012950067
ISBN: 978-0-89823-281-3
Many Voices Project #127

Cover design by Haley Frost
Author photo by Fred Schneider
Interior design by Daniel Shudlick

The publication of *Rare Earth* is made possible by the generous support of the McKnight Foundation and other contributors to New Rivers Press.

For academic permission or copyright clearance please contact Frederick T. Courtright at 570-839-7377 or permdude@eclipse.net.

New Rivers Press is a nonprofit literary press associated with Minnesota State University Moorhead.

Alan Davis, Co-Director and Senior Editor
Suzzanne Kelley, Co-Director and Managing Editor
Wayne Gudmundson, Consultant
Allen Sheets, Art Director
Thom Tammaro, Poetry Editor
Kevin Carollo, MVP Poetry Coordinator

Publishing Interns:
Katelin Hansen, Richard Natale, Katie Baker, Emilee Ruhland, and Hayley Burdett

Rare Earth Book Team:
David Binkard and Jenna Galstad

New Rivers Press
c/o MSUM
1104 7th Avenue South
Moorhead, MN 56563
www.newriverspress.com

For my parents
&
for Chris

CONTENTS

Homunculus

Milkweed	3
Trade in the New World	4
Devils 1 – Beelzebub	6
Metallurgy	7
Letter Found in an Abandoned Backpack – Mosquito Lake, Alaska	10
Devils 2 – Mephistopheles	11
Losing the Thread	12
Devils 3 – Coyote	14
Professor Plum, in the Hall, with the Rope	15
Canada Geese on the Lawn of Frasier Meadows Retirement Community	16
Devils 4 – Grendel	18
My Mother's Nipples	19

Panacea

Iron	25
My Grandmother's Rain Gauge	26
Devils 5 – Cobra	27
Chlorine	28
Arabesque	30
Devils 6 – Pan	33
Seagulls at the Local Walmart in a Landlocked State	34
Static	36
Devils 7 – Lilith	38
Sherrie's Poem	39
Nickel	41
Devils 8 – Marduk	43
Piss Yellow	44
Arsenic	46
Silicone	47

Transmutation

Gold	59
Bees	60
Devils 9 – Azazel	61
Aluminum	62
Turning Back	64
Devils 10 – Lucifer	66
Eclipse	67
Rhinestone	68
Aubade	70
Devils 11 – Void	71
Tin	72
Silver	76
NOTES	77
ACKNOWLEDGMENTS	81
ABOUT THE AUTHOR	82

If by fire
Of sooty coal th' empiric alchymist
Can turn, or holds it possible to turn,
Metals of drossiest ore to perfect gold

-John Milton,
Paradise Lost (bk 5. I. 439-42)

homunculus

Milkweed

I tell myself softly, *this is how love begins*—
the air alive with something inconceivable,
seeds of every imaginable possibility
floating across the wet grasses, under
the thin arms of ferns. It drifts like snow
or old ash, settling on the dust of the roadways
as you and I descend into thickets, flanked
by the fragrance of honeysuckle and white
primrose.

I recall how my grandmother imagined
these wanderers were living beings,
some tiny phylum yet to be classified as life.
She would say they reminded her of maidens
decked in white dresses, waltzing through air.
Even after I showed her the pods from which
they sprang, blossoming like tiny spiders,
she refused to believe.

Now, standing beside you in the crowded
autumn haze, I watch them flock, emerge from
brittle stalks, bursting upon the world as
young lovers do—trysting in the tall grasses,
resting fingers lightly in tousled hair.
Listen, and you can hear them whisper
in the rushes, gazing out at us, wondering—
what lives are these?

Trade in the New World

I.

Once the divorce went through, all parties signed,
the rains stopped. My mother, not wanting
a used-up space, moved back into the room

she'd grown up in, us with her—as from the heat
of my grandmother's attic, brown recluses unspooled
from the ceiling on ropes of silver.

As spiders wove their pocketbooks of eggs
into folds of our clothes, the dark of unused shoes,
I came to know the weight of a man—

my cheek raw with the razor-burn
of my first boyfriend. All I can recall of him now
is dread, exposure. Mother packed boxes into corners,

and each of us tucked away secrets, a sadness,
the faint whispers of crickets in wicker cages.
As I learned how flesh slowly withers around

the twin punctures, my brother Josh dreamt
in fevered sweats. Spiders would paralyze his senses,
wrap him in their silks of sleep. Mother wanted us to share

our uncle's former room. I refused—would not
share a bed. Josh cried, feeling, I'm sure,
all the more lost. How could I explain the terror

I felt—the saboteur inside saying, *Too close, too close?*
I thought I knew love's heft in my palm, its properties, formula.
What could I become? Alone in my room

I listened to Josh's terror—a life held by threads—
grow large in the dark as I spun tapestries of my own future
as I intended to live it—reclusive,

free of the ones I could stun with a kiss. In that room,
I locked a door—as under the trim of the walls,
spiders with their fiddles shuffled in.

II.

Every seven years, the cells of the body replace
themselves. We are made again, the web spun anew.
I'm not the person I was then, and therein is perhaps

forgiveness. Holidays, I travel home and Josh
greets me each time as someone new—
football player, awkward youth. What could

I say now if an account were to be made?
Only this: At a masked ball, I once met Icarus,
asked if he were an angel. Leather straps

crisscrossed the broad continent of his chest,
and behind a swath of gold satin was everything
I thought I had sought to find. I took him home

and together we beat wings across a great distance.
Come morning, all that remained was dark sea,
soft down in the sheets, and that almost forgotten

closeness—what warmth we lose in those mad
flights toward sun and the varied stars.
After a lifetime of closing doors, I let in sailors,

vagabonds, whoever could lift me from the burden
of myself, cut open the weighted purse
of a heart. To find what? A profusion of webbing?

Gold and glue-steeped feathers? Venom? How is it
I ended a boy apologizing for pattern—the logic of poison,
aerodynamics? Whatever the currency, coin, skins

for barter, it will have to be enough, and since I have it
to do over, let's be kinder to one another
in the fury . . . no, *flurry* of our failures, descents.

Devils I — Beelzebub

My time is the slow shedding of exoskeletons—
a damselfly dropping her kimono of nymph-swaddle,

sheaths of skin hung in feral halls. I've grown
so fond of pulse, sound of masticating jaws like rusty

hinges. In Babylon, with its fruit-heavy ramparts
and rot, they called me lord of insects, god of flies.

That age is over—now only legerdemain of net, sugarcoat.
At the Perth Zoo in Australia, I work in the butterfly house,

a keeper of wind-bound shamans in their mottled robes—
flame and darkness the Monarch's coat of brimstone.

That's where the stories have placed me you know, right-
hand of a throne of blood and bone. Ridiculous! Fools

make idols of fear, hand out vices like mirrors. To think
I would seek out crowns, be bested by a book and a bell.

In the Gardens, flies were company to breath, jinns
housed in the sex of orchids. Devil? Am I damned

for knowing the phases, the brief step from egg to husk—
green-backed decay, fingers dusted with sooty pastels?

No! I'm simply the one to whisper of wilt, god who named
your weakness—black angels drowned in honeyed milk.

Metallurgy

I.

Across the surfaces of tables, he leaves
no prints, the ridges of his hands long since
caulked with dark greases. In October's
dying light, my father settles like leaf-silt,
and I realize I know nothing of the workings
of his heart—a golem with gears running down,
me without knowledge of alchemy.

When we talk, we talk in metals. Lead dripping
from my tongue, silver permafrost gripped
about his eyes, copper fired in the filaments
of my hair. *This is what I have to teach,*
he says. The way iron struck with flint triggers fire.
The simplicity of brilliance, function, ore
distilled and shining with an absence of impurities.
I watch him poised over slicked innards of engines.
Blackened to elbows, he tears open cylinders
like ripe fruit, holds them up—burnt offerings
dripping nectars of oil.

My father starts the welder, a blaze of comet
erupting from his palms. Metal thaws into metal,
sends sparks around his wrists like helixes of comets.
He wears them as gods would—implacable, aloof.
What I know of metal can be summed in the hard
symmetry of my father's grasp. Callused and rigid,
soft and malleable. I try to condense him,
boil him down to something precious. With skill
he could be molded, tempered, polished to a luster
I could see myself in.

II.

In the season of comets, detritus breaks through
the atmosphere, rains down like burning manna.
After the divorce, I walk with my father
down railway tracks embroidered along the selvage
of our farm. The fields mellow with the patina
of winter diffused through their leaves.

In my first memory of fear, I watch my father,
young and sinewy as coiled wire, ride a sleek Harley
along the road beside our house. He trails
upon the landscape, as if at any instant he'll know
the secret of flight, pass away into distance.
In the trees, blackbirds cackle and open. Above is a sky
so blue everything is lost within it, and radiance speeds
toward the horizon—electric and alive.

Along this spine of iron, slag glistens in lots of stone—
cinder-like, the waste of earth when everything of use
is melted away. My father's lips glow with the slick
of misspent words—fumes of bellows passing
through his throat. Together, we search for a language
softer and bendable to the coming night.
We kick glassy resin through the demesne of lizards,
sage-faced foxes. Slag shatters on the railways
in bursts of sound, vibrant and remembered—
the pandemonium of heaven, earth.

III.

Beside the waters of Laurel Lake, swallows fold
sky into neat creases. Hunched over the opened
ribcage of our Chevy Blazer, my father tightens
battery cables—alligator clamps glinting like
gnawed lightning. I sit behind the wheel,
turning the ignition, watching as heat, dry wind,
blue of heaven forms a formula for reaction.

When the battery bursts it bathes my father's arms
in softened nuggets of gold. Running to water,
he is everything I know of security—a blaze
of watch fires lit on the hills of his skin.
A body slips under a surface of chrome,
and my father rises polished and shining.
Time will see pressure mount between us,
and our lives will be squeezed under
years stacked with decay. Already, our bones
break into shards. Who will be graphite?
Who will be diamond?

Letter Found in an Abandoned Backpack—
Mosquito Lake, Alaska

I walk the supermarket and all I can think about is you.
I paint you in portraits with lemons, mushrooms with their finned caps.

In seafood, you're laid on ice, face as red as the boiled
lobsters that conceal your nakedness. You think me so droll,

but truth is, I never believed in you. You who were made
of the dust of stars and I wanted three wishes.

In the checkout line, I read headlines of tabloids—their slanders
scribbled in red ink, *Bigfoot Takes Hiker as Sex Slave.*

Wife says, he's not the man I married. As if anything
could be so simple. It's so like me to always demand the evidence—

footprints in sand, strands of coarse hair, whitened stool.
Where is the love anymore, I want to ask. Where is the conviction?

In the woods where we walked, the prints of animals
fill with water, and the sun, reflected, blazes from

the ground like windows into other worlds. Have you
felt me move within you as you walked the inexplicable earth?

Now I look for your imprint in snow, yellow pools of urine,
for one more chance to be rare in soft beds of moss and lichen.

I never had faith enough in the real, the calamity and crush, so
is there any wonder—

I took the beast's dark hand, followed wherever you led.

Devils 2 — Mephistopheles

Some nights, the cadenzas are more than I can stand.
Strings melt to smoke, the orchestra builds to its coda.

In the wings of the Metropolitan, last night of Gounod's
Faust, the audience swoons to every laudanum-laced

aria that drips off my tongue. My old friend, I am not
immune to irony. It's been a long road for us both—

epochs since I played the *czardas* on the cat-guts,
music sizzling, sparks thrown from the bow.

Ah, you of all men know the price of conjuring chimeras,
but tonight—let's call it nostalgia—memory throws

me upon that rocky shore we call regret. Yes, even
I have felt that sting of scorpion-night. The money

rubbed together for gauze got me nothing but eternity
and a baritone. You, my friend. It was a dirty deal,

I admit—soul-skin for a fresh requiem played on fiddles
near crazed. How could anyone resist? Faust, my *amico,*

knowledge is only a gathering of questions. Winds build,
driven by brass, yet the tune sustains. You were always

my favorite. Why else take your form and voice before
the rabble to tell of your mistake? Listen! No, just listen.

Losing the Thread

For weeks, I've thought of nothing but silkworms.
    I read of them in books of industry bound

in bold, flamenco red. *The History of Global Trade.*
    I can't deny this is to escape you, appearing

on the precipice of the bed as if the answers were stashed
    in your pockets. China kept the secret of silk

from the Western world for over two thousand years.
    Eventually, Japan filched girls from silk villages,

forced out of them their trade—and a Chinese princess
    smuggled silkworm eggs and seeds of the mulberry

to Kashmir, hidden in the headdress of her gown.
    I think of silk factories in Chengdu, where ten

thousand worms feeding sounds remarkably like hard rain
    on a rooftop. In the dark, under sheets

that are not silk, nor satin or exquisite linen—my mind
    drifts to the stain of your lips, the worm-hairs

that burrow into your chest—flits to walnut trees
    in back of my parents' house, to the tent caterpillars

I mistook for those oriental weavers in their leafy troughs.
    I know you won't believe this,

but you could hear them plaiting, a sound like light sliding
    around the rims of clouds, spindles turning out a design.

Summer afternoons, I sought those canopied chambers—
    a dark mass growing at their cores,

a pumping heart of worms turning out another yarn.
    I pitched the hard hulls of unripe walnuts

into those trees, watched as larvae fell into the pungent beds
        of sage, my hand blackened

by the oils of walnut kernels. So you see my crime,
        having raided the palaces at the top of the world,

taken the eggs of the ancient worm, that seed of invention,
        silks of every color—ecru, cantaloupe, dew.

So what can I say folded out of those fabrics—
        the needed story of how our loves knot?

No, that plunder was not the cost of desire,
        but the end—love the missile, cocked and fired,

the siege begun. Isn't it always like this, the egg
        and seed together? Does it matter which came first?

Devils 3 — Coyote

So what's it going to be? Beast or thumbprint
of star-flesh? An old question—whether to fuck

or filter sky from the crusts we come to. For me,
it is a moot point—nerves uttering a yelp too ear-

splitting to deny. I remember when I lent you fire,
exposed where it lay sealed in Wood's bone-work.

Sex to you is canyon-cleft, mountain-spar, too close
to earth for your comfort. I have slept with all your

women. Just ask them. They'll tell you of the one
who stroked them in the dream-walk, who ripped

through the catcher's cobwebs. And where were you?
With your eyes again tuned to heaven, hunting the mythic

eagle you term control? Men should think more often
with their organs—or are you so vain as to believe

this life, with its sweats and gut purges, is some gauntlet
to immensity. I am here to call you back into the night.

For there's a price to fire—how it infects, burns from
tongue-tip to testicles, drips like wax from your sex.

Life is a match-head touched to a short fuse, yet you
piss to put it out. Let it burn. Let it ravage the world.

Professor Plum, in the Hall, with the Rope
~ after Meg Kearney

The board balanced on a stack of phone books, my first crush
        Jason Belson and I scrutinize each other over
swabbed interiors, aristocracy, weapons. We search the house for clues.

In the ballroom, Mr. Green, who's been shtupping Jason's mother
        for seven months, slips a chapped hand
under her scarlet dress.

Over her slim shoulder, Green's eyes are emerald-slits of murder.
        He kisses the tips
of her fingers, his lips wetted with nicotine as they dip,

nearly puddling on the floor. Jason plucks a crimson feather from her dress,
        marks her as suspect. "She's such a whore," he accuses
within hearing. The suspect doesn't bat a lash.

Mustard, home from a double, sits for hours
        in the kitchen, lights out. The Colonel can smell
his wife's cigarettes from across the house.

Later, he will ascend the stairwell, soft-footed, scratch
        his way into his wife's room, and choke her. Counting
each second, one-by-one, until he's sure she remembers how much

she needs him. Jason has taken to hiding behind doors.
        In his fists he twists pipes and candlesticks
until his palms are raw and cracked.

"All of this is strictly confidential," he tells me. "I started a game
        where I hide knives about the house. I leave them
until I've forgotten where they are. Surprise me."

In my mind, I've checked off the rooms where I've wanted it to happen—
        on the pool table in the billiard room,
chaise lounge in the study. Jason's naked hand

reaching from the shadows, pressing my mouth shut—
        the perfect crime—
no one noticing when the board is put away, there are pieces missing.

Canada Geese on the Lawn of Frasier Meadows Retirement Community

First snow of the season, they're out
in the cold. Aged ladies in shawls
wrapped tight against the chill,

heads tucked against their breasts.
Slowing the car, flurries are driven
in tangos across blacktop as I watch them

congregate about the rose beds, a social
of women gathered for gardening. Can they
not feel weather in their bones

prickle like a hard frost? They pilfer
the undersides of ornamental kale
for corms, crocuses, the bright memory

of a season past. Late roses on their
toothy stems are gripped in fists of ice.
Dimes of locust leaves drop with the weight

of winter at their backs. Has no one come
for these women, gathered at their task,
pulling at grasses as if fortunes could be told

by the fall of blades on a cold plate?
Auguries drift from sky in a tattered letter
from the gods, and rough time lies

slipped about the roots of bare cottonwoods
beside the pond—its skin of duckweed
going brittle from the outside in.

Gossip rises from their throats
with life of its own—a hiss of spittle
on an iron. One look and it's obvious,

they're sounder than we'd care to think.
Slowly the quilts stack about them,
stitches tight, the remembered patterns—

Ruins of Jericho, World Without End.

Devils 4 — Grendel

Have none of you pity for the ancient? In the fens,
death stacks upon death, and from this comes

a kind of life. Born of marsh gas, and returned by hand
of human king, you can never be done of me. Having

neither human face nor heart—I am not the fiend
nor devil. I am the monster—divine portent of flesh's

failure, slurred by your naming. Choose a catastrophe,
any burning holocaust, and tell me what form of creature

you find crawling there. And for what? To move
the kingdom another hectare forward? To piss your scent

on another defeated people? Did it ever occur to you
the world may not want you? Once I was unique,

and for this I was wronged. My severed head dropped
into stagnant silence by that beautiful boy, and then,

mere spore-factory, truffles tucked under skin of soil.
From death, there's only the cycle of dispersal—the comfort

to be taken from how we molder. Know this—all epics
have endings, the bards' songs splinter in their throats.

Be you dragon-slayer or son of gods, you will hear my howl—
all that is left of me—and know what it is you come to.

My Mother's Nipples

~ after Robert Hass

I. How Not to Write a Poem about Your Mother's Nipples

Don't say she's the font of all life.
Don't say the life force was a thread spun from the tip—Rumpelstiltskin's golden
    straw.
Don't compare them to fruit. Ever.
Don't vicariously caress, stroke, nuzzle, suckle, pinch, bite, jiggle or man-handle
    them. That's your mother for Christ's sake.
Which reminds me. Don't compare them to famous breasts of history. They are in no
    way similar to Godiva's bouncing at a gallop. Nor Joan of Arc's seared bright
    as bloodstones. They're not even in the same league as Madonna's (modern
    or ancient).
Don't skirt the issue entirely, touching them like a hand-slapped boy who runs to the
    dark of the woodshed to cry.
Don't resurrect past lovers who thumbed them for a time, and then moved on to
    greener pastures and rounder globes, leaving her adrift in her shining until she
    moored in the bay of your life.
Leave off all mention of your current lovers. Even after several drinks at the local bar,
    when the bartender, Barry, shows you his nipple rings, and you get the urge to
    chew them until someone begs for mercy, until those red suns set or rise or
    nova, don't mistake this ache for a nipple that was taken and never returned to
    you.
Avoid the pornographic. Obviously.
Don't be truthful. Don't admit they are something so remote and alien you could not
    pick them out of a lineup. Could not find them in the rubbish of an antique shop.
Don't admit that if language were adequate, you could pull out a single word, lucid
    and clean, that would echo a memory so close and warm and liquid.

II. Conception

I would like it to have been a summer evening,
the pickup's windows down, the air outside loud and alive.

I'd like to believe the last sliver of daylight
was just a place she was leaving, traveling down an alley

through cornfields, the scent rich in the cab.
My father would have his arm around her shoulder, the other

on the wheel. On second thought, no. Something riper,
fraught with impatience. His hand is warm between

her thighs. Ahead, the lake is a lighter shade
of night between the trees, the moon whittling itself

into those waters. She is thinking of the wet hearts
of watermelons, the sutures of bats over the docks.

The radio would be playing John Cougar—"Paper in Fire."
Or a song she won't remember the name of, containing a girl,

a lonely highway, desert sand, and a need so careless
it could cut you in two. My father would have by now

parked the truck on a rise overlooking the lake. His hair
shaggy and thick, his body a thin, rawhide whip—

just like in the photos, the tips yellow with age.
When he touches her, something within her

would loosen and want to move. She would feel his lips
graze her shoulder. His hands open her shirt.

She would be thinking about snowmelt, the roughness
of his hands. How her breasts were small birds,

barely plumaged, blinking, amazed at being naked
and newly in the world. She would think paper moons,

magnolia, gypsy moths, and want him to set them aflame.

III. Sentimentality

She said they nearly fell off.
Nursing two sons, their mouths a need
she could never seem to satiate,
pulled and bitten to hard buttons.

She was never so aware of them—
the scratch of nylon, raw at the tips.
Tenderness is what she called it.

She never felt so animal—
her body going liquid, milky with every
thin breeze, every helpless cry.

The hounds in back of the house
bayed, and her breasts beaded
a new moon for each and everyone.

IV. What Is Left

After two days of March heat, the forsythia is a woman come early to the party, dressed to kill. Yellow silk. For seven days now, I have tried to write about my mother's nipples. The lawns have since put on their green jerseys. Every bud tipped—red and spun from the branch's tight hollow. The shape of spring is spiral, the movement out.

If I close my eyes, I sometimes think I can picture them. Not as they are now, but earlier. Chevrons advancing through the blue wool of her sweater. She is standing in sunlight. No bra, the sweater becoming too hot in the early highs. Maybe she's just had words with her mother, fled the house to feel for a moment larger in the world. Everything around her is about to push itself raw, and if she grasps the low branches of her mother's pear tree she knows the taste and heft of those late summer globes will rise in her throat. The texture of the thing. Tight skin. The meat crisp. Her fingers wet and sticky. She hears her mother's voice saying, *I'll send you off if ever I think I can't handle you. For your own good.* She's thinking of a boy she's seeing as she moistens the tips of her fingers, runs them up under her sweater to her nipple. On the highway, trucks lumber by spinning chrome scintilla, speeding toward parts unknown. The map's edge. Toward a bright, bright future.

My mother grew up in a family of five brothers. She married and had three sons. When her mother had a stroke and died, it was as if one breast had been cut away, and she could still feel the itch of it where it no longer rested under her shirt. She searched the house for it. In the cupboards, the potato chest, behind the magazine rack. She searched boxes of her mother's things. What to keep? What to give away? It wasn't until months later she found it again. In a changing stall in J.C. Penney, trying on blouses of unyouthful colors, she looked up and there it was. Pink and bashful in the light, its shape no prize-winner to be sure, but it was there. Her mother's inheritance. She walked out of the stall holding it. She passed the salesgirls folding slips, the pear-shaped security guard, holding it. All the way home, past the white churches, the hills polluted with wildflowers, holding it. Past the roadside booths selling honey, grape tomatoes, holding it. All the while thinking *dear life. For dear life.*

panacea

Iron

In the summer of my sixteenth year, I fell in love with Auden.
My parents, newly divorced, walked away from each other—
Mother and I moved into my grandmother's two-story
brick-stone. That year, the locusts swarmed. Their slender,

grass-blade bodies crashed at the windows. Nights I slept
in my Uncle Rich's former room, the windows up, listening
to the rasp of legs on the screen—the slow,
rhythmic strum of life. I'd wait until the house was still,

then pull out the magazines my uncle left in a trunk
beneath a stack of quilts stale with the smell of old sun.
Upon the glossy pages, women with perms and cherry-stain
press-on nails spread-eagled. Their legs and arms twined

around the cool steel of men, skin dark as teased leather.
With a pair of my grandmother's sewing scissors,
I cut away the feminine from around the metal.
Legs and torsos met with empty spaces, every candy apple

nail pried from stiff cocks and discarded.
What was left? Slabs of ore in my fist, paper dolls
with too many legs. I taped those men into a scrapbook.
Every page, burnished iron. I cut away what life offered,

detaching the undesired. Yet it's hard to contain merely bodies
to a book. So much more creeps in at the edges—connotation,
nicks of a double-bladed tool, shadows of the ones cut away.
In the summer quiet, Auden's verse was sweat—

with sudden, swift emergence come the women in dark glasses,
the hump-backed surgeons and the scissor-man.
I was never confused by Auden's dark stranger. Winter came,
locusts fell like star-shrapnel, and as I learned the words of sieges—

divorce, death, faggot, AIDS—the scissor-man was there,
antiseptic gloves, scalpel. He took them away. With each slice,
me barely under, he whispered into the anesthesia like a lover.
Oh, what a troubadour. Oh, what a pair we make.

My Grandmother's Rain Gauge

To read it, she needs only a trifle of gear—
a tarnished gamecock blowing
racket from the gable roof, a glass
cylinder on a finger of cedar. She's
familiar with weather's levy, the storm's
rough bluster and charge. After rain,
she trundles her masticated body
to the measure, her eyes long
milked of vision. She cannot read
the grim numbers ascending to the lip,
but she knows what light on water
looks like—studied from the mercury
of a hundred children's fevers.
She knows weather like the back of her fist—
flood unlacing banks of ferns,
dawn laminating icicles on the eaves.
Just like the morning she gave herself
to her husband—the first time,
when saline ran from her in swells.
Since his death, she's run tallies
on the stream, drinking by inches the loss.
She's kept account of what's owed her.

Devils 5 — Cobra

Nietzsche said, "The only God worth believing
in is a dancing God," and in this regard, I have

not failed you. In the heat-brittle bazaars of Jaipur,
hawkers vend jute bags, ajwan seeds, henna oil—

their shouts boiled in the liquid wind. It's with this life,
avatar of the serpent, that I come to understand you.

We're a dying breed, you and I—a god in this sheaf
of scales dumbstruck by your fingers on the gourd flute.

When in the woven night you came with black
thread and needle, sewed my mouth like a slit purse,

I knew your fear as if it were my own, your need
of music without risk, the hood's black diamond a burden

you would not bear, even for a glimpse of that bastion
in the sky. In the sibilance of teeming streets the kathakali

begins sinuous in the limbs of festooned girls, as I
pitch with the spell of the tune wand. In any dance

there is a tilt. Tethered to the rolling sphere, we are
punch-drunk—come closer, my charge. This forked

tongue will lick your threads to cinder. Watch close,
keep time—the steps of this dance will come to you.

Chlorine

The clubhouse pool shimmers—afternoon light.
Dragonflies still themselves above blue water,

their wings thin as paper held on the rising
heat. Chris and I stand to either side
of his daughter as the other tenants stare,

whisper. Two men, barely beyond boyhood,
with a little girl—*Where's the mother,*
they murmur, sound like the approach of rain

across the cupped palms of leaves. Not a solace
coming, but a burden. I can't explain—early pregnancy,

a marriage over before it had begun, or that Chris'
ex-wife sits stoned in a motel across town, that she sent
Courtney home with a head infested with lice.

Here we let the crisp chlorine do what it can—
soak the snags of hair, turn back the incursion.
In the warm envelope of fluid, we coax Courtney

to tilt back her neck, a baptism to wash away memory.
Stubbornly, she pulls back, fearful we'll let her go.

We make promises no one expects us to keep,
and her head goes under. Brass filaments fan
in a liquid element. She rises, beads strung

through her bangs, rockets of daylight
broken on the water. As the three of us gather
our towels, let the rough threads take in moisture,

I collect Courtney into my arms. Her skin smells
of coconut and chlorine. Sometimes this life feels

like a going-over. The wreckage of our lives adrift,
gulls picking through flotsam for the chum, as we tuck
what floats under our arms and set adrift.

From her hair, I take a louse between forefinger
and thumb, press hard until it breaks. I do what I can—
wash the blood away, part tangles, continue searching.

Arabesque

I.

Sometimes the world leaves a remark.
Walking the borders of this cornfield where mud
laps at the legs of hickories, there are places
where rain collects, drainage like
a lacquered serpent through the grass. At the sun's
descent, light strikes every weed-stem like a torch,
and in the mire, under the shade of a sycamore,
tracks are cast in drying clay—rakings
of raccoons and the twin half moons of deer.
What earth leaves me—pods of milkweed,
snakeskin, the steel, fluted feathers of crows.
I learn how to trail these indentions,
the etchings terrain leaves like a cipher
we overlook—salt lick,
warren, wind break of piñon like dark
water on the hills. Language from the grammar—
our words to this world and the next.

II.

Before her death, my grandmother cut
a swathe through the pasture to the back ponds.
You could track her progress by bends in
the sedge, their stems like broom bristles
sweeping at the sky. The Jerseys
slouched in the mudflats and the murky
waters winked their clouded eyes—irises
the ghost-ripples of startled wood ducks,
the skipped stones of algae-backed turtles.
She disappeared in a late afternoon,
into dusty light with a silver bowl tucked
under her arm, the strong unguents of Jimson
whipped by wind, and returned at dusk
with an armful of night-fruit—black and dew-
berries, muscadines, tight-skinned persimmons,
and salads like sheets of parchment.
To follow her meant curving as she did
around the kinks of blackberry brambles.
She slipped into the cutting hedge,
and I learned quickly how to judge the tangle.
How to interweave body with thorn and flower,
come out the other side into a hidden
and fruitful queendom. I can still see her hand
reaching for those black pearls, wood
opals grown on a pit. This is how it was when
she died. Some nights, I dream of catching her
in the patch, doused and hidden in the moonlight.
She looks up, shanks quivering, runs to a path
overgrown with sumac, cattail, witch-hazel—
strange prints leading into darkness.

III.

Nineteen. I'm standing in a riot
of field flowers—Shasta daisies and goldenrod.
My boyfriend gathers weeds by the bushel
for his sister's wedding to the sheriff's son.
Who better to gather blister and red clover than us
gay boys with our silken tastes.
She wants the church shrouded, the blooms'
slim fingers upturned in prayer—bearing witness.
My grandmother's casket was like a parcel
rearing white-glove lilies, asters, snapdragons.
It's been a season since we buried her, her plot
off Highway 65 shaded by mimosas.
So much has happened in her absence,
and grief—like so many things—is like a banking
swallow. The wing-blades turn and suddenly
there's a bleeding cut from the blue.
In the alpha curve of vine, the chaos pattern
of an overrun pasture, my footfalls are sounder.
The price is the losing—the tracks
leading nowhere, rust on the patterned leaf,
the pushed-down beds of grass.
In the Jeep, on the way back to town,
Chris' hand kneads the knot of muscle in my thigh.
Heat wilts the flowers, and their pollen grimes
my arms—a golden spread from the meadowlands.
I consider sucking it from Chris' fingers. But I know
it'll taste of dust—and I haven't learned yet
how to savor that elixir.

Devils 6 — Pan

Myth has held, after the glory, a mariner tracing
the selvage of Greece heard a bird-cry pronouncing

my death. I am not dead. Befuddled, perhaps,
a century or more on a glut of claret and women—

reawakened to find my name slandered. A demon
you call me, with cloven hoof, curved cock. I'll admit

to two of those. Do you need me, my kids, to lay blame
to your tepid thirsts? What do any of you know

of the pasture's edicts, its staunch demands? I was here
at the beginning—my reed pipe hauled you from black

mud. Where is the shame in this? You demand
too much, the stars above so far from your reach

you gave them the value of all. Remember my works
when you slip from your pinched cloisters, song

stirring the jelly of your brains in this mountain urn.
In the noonday silence, when panic ravages you

in columbines, thistles a horror in the fields, look for
the signs that will mark me—smell of civet and urine,

hooves beating melody to this lust you left to the wild,
swaddled in fleece. I am the shepherd, you are the feral.

Seagulls at the Local Walmart in a Landlocked State

Description: 23-26" (58-66 cm). Large gull. Adults dirty pearl to white; black wingtips speckled, louse-colored. From tip to tip, an unfolded map. Feet fleshy, but will appear scaled. Bills yellowish to rust-orange-pliers-on-a-dock. Eyes brutish, exiled—resembling soap opera matrons, past their prime and greedy, who pour tears into martinis every night.

Voice: Hoarse squawk, guttural, swallowed gravel, crushed glass, hooks, fast-food wrappers, tobacco butts, grease. Some sound remarkably like children. *Kuk-Kuk-Kuk, Yucca-Yucca-Yucca.*

Habitat: Coastlines of lakes, oceans. Banks of rivers, estuaries, canals. Flocks gather in parking lots. Strange they should be so inland. They gather and scatter in air—litter-strewn; scraps of messages never found in their bottles. Sometimes they mistake the handicap spaces for ocean, and they'll stand there, all facing the same way, windward, waiting for the hard soup under their legs to boil.

Range: Spreading. Up either coast—Alaska to palm-plagued Manzanillo. Greenland to the temperate islands. They stow away on trailers and are seeded. Landfills, shopping centers. Acolytes of American avarice. Spilt sugar to vegetable skin to the calm waters of concrete. Sometimes they dive into it, smashing their brains to jelly.

Nesting: Lays spotted, olive-tan eggs in nests of seaweed or dead grass. Usually found among cliffs or dunes. Hard-boiled, sprinkled with paprika, they are delectable. In a pinch, they will build nests anywhere. Shopping carts, unattended children's car seats, the faces of storefronts. They often build in colonies. Between the splayed hands of W. The neat compartments and shelters of A & M.

Comments: Scavengers; they will swallow winter, isolation, deportment. Even death. Especially death. The savor reminds them of home. Fish-bellied, mollusks, trash, aquatic stars, medical waste. They often steal. This watcher has seen one pluck a compact from the hand of a young girl, hair like kelp in the wind. It must have mistook it for a clam. It took it up among the low clouds and dropped it. The lot of them gathered for the meat, but found nothing but fleshy powder. A fatty swab that stained their features. By the sounds of them, they are growing angrier and angrier by the day.

Static

I never understood you, stopping to pluck wads of thread
caught in the carpet, pinching lint from the wash.
If control could be measured in dryer sheets, you could have
synchronized the world, separating the light from dark.

I never understood how you lived with me, knowing my favorite
color was gray. Knowing I rubbed the world
against me until I was static—ready to spark.

I picked up everything the air offered for kindling,
fuel for the combustion I felt in the spaces of my ribs—
small fires you tended and hedged in the small of my back.

Driving through town, you show me places you've known.
The white suburban house, your grandmother's,
crouched behind 4 o'clocks and tiger lilies.
The grade school where the playground rusted in the rain.

You point out a house on the east side of town, perched
on the roadside like a black eye, and disclose how
once you steered past it in the night, looking for your mother.
Making sure she was safe inside with the other addicts.

Your grandmother gives her three months to live. Doctors
lengthen the diagnosis like a crocheted afghan—patient and slow.
First, endocarditis and hep C stolen like kisses
from needles, then liver failure—the body freebased.

Your mother calls. The two of you chat about medications,
the pain behind her eyes. When you hang up,
you try to remember whether or not you were brave,
or knew the right things to say.

                              Later, lying in the curve
of your body, we talk—lay out what secrets we can.
You speak of your mother, how you would find her
strung out on hands and knees, picking through the lint
of the carpet, looking for a rock.
                         How is it I can't find any grief,
you ask, drawing me closer into the dark. *It will come*, I say.
Even now, it hangs in spaces closest to the ceiling, like cool
light of fireflies fleeing through your fingers—or like lint

left in the bed between us, disregarded until taken up,
pulled apart, unwound, unknotted, exposed for what it is.

Devils 7 — Lilith

Sometimes the Garden was witch-grass, kaffir lily,
anemone—and sometimes it wasn't. Sometimes

the names came like smoke, others like water.
If you think it woman's work to bend in the garden,

then Adam was a cunt. I have moved through so many
mirrors in this life, I no longer have to look to find

my lips. To fit in this current age one must be steel,
crow's feet. We have all of us sinned in pride.

I wanted life in excess, the garden gone to seed.
You wanted the zephyr baptized in petrol, cum

upon, and bridled. No! It can't begin like this
again—knives drawn, wrists tied. There's something

I have to say to you. When I left Eden, it hurt you,
how I coupled with the common and unlighted,

how your bright face was never reflected in theirs.
So we named again in the clearing—whore, limp

dick, prick-tease, Daddy's boy. You weren't an easy
man to suffer, and I, no garden variety. Sometimes

it was raindrop-brilliant, bat-fur-softness, lamb's wool.
Sometimes it wasn't. Our mistake, to ignore this sadness.

Sherrie's Poem

Sometimes love leaves us with a lot of tinder,
handfuls of ash stirred by the broad wings of birds.
From the house, light trickles from the windows,
                                              aglow,
warming the silhouettes of gaunt lovers—
stirred like shades in search of dark corners, a doorway.

In my mind, I see you best by firelight.
In back of Michael's old Victorian
with the hole in the gable where fire had tried its escape.

Yet, it's not that flame I recall, but another—
where you gathered dead limbs from under the sycamores
and built them into a pyre. A month after the breakup,
Jennifer, your lover of eleven years,
left you with more books than could be carried away.

We joked that you could build a house with them,
but instead you took a book of Neruda's love poems,
a pulp novel of lesbian erotica,
and parked your RV in a rut that was once a garden
behind Michael's home, history tucked
under the bottlebrush and myrtles.

There you built a fire. To nourish it, you served
it lines of sonnets. *I want to eat the fleeting shade
of your lashes . . . In the center of the earth I will push
aside the emeralds so that I can see you . . .*

Michael said it was vanity or something.
He left us there amid smoke and the evening's hum,
retreating to his dying lover, David,
whom I never saw, out of sight in the house,
wired and bested by the morphine and protease inhibitors.

Through the light cast, bats pleated, pursuing
the tiniest of things. You acquainted me with the family
of owls nested behind the RV. How they alighted
on low branches at sunset and watched as you built

a space of consumption—lit candles against mosquitoes
bred in the holes of elms, all to burn the bandanna
given to you by Jennifer on your eight year anniversary—
watched as flame took, as blue heat licked at the edges
and curled them in a blackness you could fold a heart into.

Nickel

Weekends in my youth, my grandmother took me
to the quiet lawns of churches. There, with the blunt-

ended rod of a metal detector, we swept bundles
of grass-straw and grave-shadow for burnished

remnants—musket balls sieved from the barrels
of old conflict, coins rare and tendered

with cryptograms most have forgotten. She sold
them at flea markets to oily-eyed men with briefcases

full of useless memory. Above us, steeples
lanced into the gears of storm-engines, as below

I learned the supple music the world makes. My job
was to dig, to wonder what new possibility waited

to be opened, as my grandmother deciphered sonic
notes echoed from turf. She told me, *Each form*

of metal carries its own tone—as if it wished to speak
its name. With heads bent close to the land,

we listened for the rasp of silver, muted grunts
of copper, and the harsh pitch of what was heavy—

iron, steel, brass. Never knowing what would unearth,
bottle caps, caches of stones, or the doors and gate-

locks of some *El Dorado,* that near-believed-in city
of gold. Unnamable darkness became a form of faith

more tangible than the whitewashed temples I crawled
beneath, spade in hand. Later that summer, toward

evening in my grandmother's backyard, while fireflies
burned like pinpricks in celluloid, I divined the only

treasure I could call my own—a nickel with the solid
weight of a buffalo on its back. My grandmother

polished it in vinegar, gave it back a moon-touched
luster, and told me how I should count the legs

of the beast, saying coins minted with three were
unique, worth more for their lack. What I took

from these lessons—that at every moment miracles
are forged, twisted, and forgotten—overlooked

in dull dust. They wait to be found, dark three-legged
forms—their handicaps near unnoticed in the gallop.

After my grandmother's death, I sat at her graveside.
All around grew flowers without scent, upturned

saucers of color beaming to an unsearched sky.
Wind chimes placed on a garland rang in the air,

and I mistook them for a language of faith.
The silver cameo and gold band she was buried

with—singing their lullabies, passwords ceded
through the keyhole of a bullioned city. I ran

my hand over the trimmed grass, felt a vibration.
Not knowing what to seek, I dug into the husk of it—

dimmed flicker of history, miracle of how we go on.

Devils 8 — Marduk

After time, I learned to quell the blood-thirst with
a quicksilver syringe, and on these streets I diminish.

Once a storm-god above Babylon, now an addict
nursing a vein—it was your voice that summoned

me from the surge of hawthorns, your dancing maidens
in their sky-toned satins. Enchanted, I lent you key

to the Garden, and you built of it dominion—your hand
hooking life to dirt. Send me back. This concrete's colder

than mountain snow. I should've stayed in the meadowland,
but the girls in the temple-quiet kissed jubilation.

Later, when priests cut open my belly and inserted a furnace,
how could I not take them, limbs of alabaster, sandalwood?

The reek of sacrifice is a pall of ravens on a desert sky.
Slung from the dark-empty with its myriad cries, I wanted

nothing but company—to stand and suckle your throb,
such noise in the seed-case. But the temples slumped

to their knees and the blood ran out. I wandered to Saigon,
found the cud of opium, and tried to forget your taste.

I have worried this tit to powder, and still in dreams
pushers come with bleeding virgins—such life, such need.

Piss Yellow

On the morning of All Hallow's Eve,
you turn at waking and tell me she's going to die.

A thousand miles away, your mother spits
blood into a burnished basin. Her liver, now pitted

rubbish from a life of surfeit, has given up the ghost,
and the unfiltered piss brews in her body—

a steeped and chthonic tea. Later, you and I stagger
into the pasture's stillness, leaves drifting like burned

paper on the wind. The fields are banshee-dressed;
ice glinting in ape of the stars. Evening gathers

itself—shadows mount at the sun's descent
and the sheared nubs of cornstalks rise like broken

leg-bones of deer. Above us, the water tower's
beacon brushes the muslin of melting snow, molded

in abstractions of women. Some hunger takes you.
The world becomes a coin of light, continually tossed

and landing on its edge. You crave a human taste—
mother's milk, albumen, firm grease, salt,

anything to remind you how to mourn her.
How to forgive the gun she pressed into your hand

en route to a house where you sat in the car,
the gun heavy in your lap—too scared to step out

of the car to piss as you waited for her shadow
at the window. *Why now,* you ask,

as if such answers were waiting just beyond
the reach of light in the dark. Even still, the signal

from the tower swings, the boats unmoor—
the keeper, in his glass gable, watches from shore.

Arsenic

It's been a hard spell. Christmas leaves a trail
of tinsel and twisted hooks snared in the carpet,

and still the air outside sweats against the glass.
At four years old, Courtney understands the season

as the changing colors of circuited lights, swirls
of ribbon laid out under the tree like roots.

She seizes the fragile green and silver balls
Chris gives her, places them on the tree in clusters.

I go behind, spread them out along the branches.
In her father's arms, Courtney places the angel

at the top of the tree. She turns, smiles as if she questions
nothing in this world—not peace, not me.

It's been a week since she came back from her mother's,
revealed how the neighbor touched her while

her mother was at work. After two years, my breath
still catches whenever she tears around sharp corners,

tilts into the turns. I feel as helpless as this tree leaned
in the corner—dried, caustic, a mere alliance of tinder—

or like this ever-futile angel. Courtney's eyes catch
the glow of tallow, and I rise as she takes me in her arms,

rests me at the peak of a shock of needles.
There have been false starts, tumbles from innocence

to stand here—leaning earthward, a candle gripped
in my fist, like everything I have failed to contain.

Silicone

I.

With day's slow heat, we return to the bar
where we met. You drink Crown, while I slug back
jewelers' hammers. Over rum shots, I tell
you I'm leaving for school in fall. You say,
Let's drink to love. Earlier, Michael called
for a chauffeur to the Silicone Ball.
Not knowing what he meant, I agreed.
Already, bulbs of breasts, like chanterelles, peek through
his shirt. You scoff into your drink, amber-
light, heady fumes. The smell of ambergris
wafts from your wrist. You say, *Even gay men
should act like men*, then grab your cock and pull—
a gesture I find entrancing, cheeky.
Pressed beneath these sheets of days, I give in.

II.

Dream a siege of birds-of-paradise, you'd
come close—spears of feathers gored in claret,
tears of lapis. In the motel, drag queens
arrange themselves on chairs, sit Indian-
style on the lips of beds. Driving over
in the car, Michael tells me he'll soon be
a woman. Waiting in the cool of the room,
circled by shows of royalty, I think
of you. Before leaving, you asked if we'd
weathered the storm. I never answered.
Masks grin from all sides. An ever-growing
absence patterns the windows—burns of frost.
Deception is an honest show at living—
ask any queens in ersatz tiaras.

III.

After four rounds of shots, you slur words.
Say things like, *We'll keep in touch, love can dare
distance.* I say, *We should see other people.
Two years will feel a lifetime.* Through smoke,
vivid globes ricochet across felt lawns.
A man, in a second-skin of jeans, chalks
his stick. Stacks of quarters glow like moons.
You motion, *We could take him home, just to see.*
I catch what's meant, but before I say, *Yes,*
something gives within me. Outside, trees drop
color. Our table a wreck—glass and swill.
You skin labels off bottles of beer, slit them
to tatters, then arrange them on the bar
like a conundrum. You point and summon.

IV.

These are not social creatures. Yet they come
with their needs etched in hard lines of jaws.
Light grips the tight architecture of cheeks.
They wait, bejeweled hands held placid in pools
of their laps, cake of make-up hardening.
Mistress Sable arrives. I watch as she takes
from her bag a syringe, clear bottles
of silicone. For hard cash she injects
cheeks, hips and lips, anywhere you covet—
fill out taut until curves manifest.
What's wanted is ability to change.
Come one, come all, Sable says. *I have my*
anodynes and potions, buoyancy in carafes.
Sable knows, sugar, light can be so harsh.

V.

He struts to our table—ivory bull,
ivory swan. Grace and belligerence.
His name is Paul. You throw on charm, a red
garland. We present ourselves, give false names.
Through the impossible white of his shirt,
nipples like buttons insinuate.
It's hard, this tendency toward the new, never
been tasted. Something was mislaid here.
Already, this loss like an amputee's itch,
junkies for a needed solace—a fleeting
fix. You look to me for direction.
I blow kisses as we three exit the door.
Outside, solid weather, west wind whistles
right through us. Hollow echo, hallowed horn.

VI.

Michael grips my fist as needle goes in.
Pants around his knees, his prick like a pulled-
up root, Michael winces as gleaned earth
adheres to his thigh. Sable titters at his
cringe, swats at the tuber distended
between his legs. *Shame to split somethin' so
ripe.* Michael beams. Before arriving, we
gossiped about Sable's past. How she was
barred from the bright stages of Atlanta
for sneaking crushed glass into the compacts
of her competition. *She's had a rough life.
Like me,* Michael says. His shadow lengthens,
hips swell to birthing. He's stillborn—still
changing. Scrotum pulls up, tucks itself inside.

VII.

How should I speak of raw desire? Let's say,
underneath the skin of denim, wolf-scent.
Pores pressed lip-to-lip form wet chambers, cells.
Out of blue, this trinity and too much
sensation. Bristles of your face are flecks
of lodestone, while novel calluses press
the small of backs. Three threads make intricate
knots. Then, startling climax—veins fired
in the eyes like flares, burning syringes.
After, fading idols exit at the door,
and then alone with you. In my mind is
a crawl space barely four feet wide. Something
inside decides to fail, to come undone.
I need an image. A clean show of faith.

VIII.

I met Michael working at a subs shop.
He was what we called *obvious. Hopeless.*
First night, he told me he was a woman
trapped in the case of man. Later, closing,
he confides that at thirteen, his mother
sold him to a carny for the price
of a fix. *She was a junkie from way back.*
The carny ran a lemonade stand for
roving fairs. Days, Michael squeezed bitterness
into cups. At night, the carny groped him
in the dark, smell of citrus like sunshine.
It wasn't all bad. Sometimes he liked it,
would pluck his eyebrows to reedy lines for
the Lemon Man, expression of surprise.

IX.

Morning after, I wake to find you gone.
In panic, I fail to hear the shower,
steam from the bath sewed with the fragrance
of exotic tinctures—apricot, star fruit.
Suddenly, it's too much. The familiar—
morning's pink hush, sparks of riffraff in light,
the sound of you one room over. Distinct,
yet accessible. Joining you as you
lather the tableau of your chest, froth breath-
less at the tips of your hair, there is this
moment of nothing to say. I reach out,
dust the tip of a nipple. Sheepishly,
you grin. I've seen this a hundred times.
It decants my heart, like the first time, the last.

X.

In the dresser mirror, flashing lights from
neon outside dress the room in pinks, blues.
Sable packs her things as queens turn their prize,
inflamed faces into view of the glass.
Michael rubs his hips like magic lamps.
Effects are startling, how so little can do
much. *Look at this,* he says. *Hourglass!*
He walks to me, waist rolling like a rough sea—
and it's as if he's real for the first time
under his skin. My chest half-lifes to dark
matter, the something that's always nothing—
love, loneliness, guilt. Sable turns to leave,
and I run to plead for that needle,
for spaces within me needing to be filled.

transmutation

Gold

Light, and then the failing of light, are all the bees
know of time. Detonations of pear blossoms,
noon sun, thoraxes gilded with pollen,
the silent flowers—all mere barter of the hive.

In the brood nest, grubs catch gifts of nectar—
workers dance through lacy territories of the comb.
What do any of them know of contention?
What cravings could test them at their songs?

Through the wild meadow bees arc like arrows
over moving grasses, sprays of proliferate weed.
Could you imagine a life as simple and unriddled,
risen to your time in a season of beeswax,

sugarcoat, luciferous clarity—whatever you will?

Bees

There were bees behind the walls
of my grandmother's home,
and they lived there more
comfortably than she ever did.

After her husband died, she fell
lax in the housework. Wouldn't
scrub floors or dust the mantle—
only took up a hoe if there were
snakes in the begonias.

She traveled to yard sales every
Sunday, pilfering the rubbish
of other people's lives.
She carried it home in carloads,
slowly filling the empty rooms
with wax and hardened honey.

The first space to go was the bedroom.
Memories were crowded out
by a host of tiny porcelain dogs,
polyester blouses, wickerwork.

With the gaps filled in, the house
became livable once more. Spiders
filled the bathtub, mice took
up the floors, the bees tangoed
in the walls. When we lured
my grandmother away, she left with a
pittance of unremarkable things.

The house was condemned and my
father deemed it best to let it burn.
Aflame, it sizzled for hours. The bees,
disturbed in their dances, flew out
of the walls on fire—blazing for
an instant and lessening to cinder.

Devils 9 — Azazel

When I left the desert, humankind had nearly
forgotten me. No longer did the goats with their hides

soaked in sin of the tribe wander into my coffer.
Nowadays, I work in a Paris jeweler, huddled over the labor

of lapidaries—palms made luminous by star rubies,
jade and diamonds. When you came at last to the desert,

sandstorms had rubbed the rocks to supine postures,
and that's perhaps how it happened. A maiden bathing

naked in the delta captured my thirst, and I lured her
with bead-pearls to my shade. In the night's cool, her body

oasis, I taught her how to paint herself—
kohl like a threshold to the eyes, scent of eucalyptus

rubbed at the nape of neck. She left once my mystery
had faded, returned to her people weighted with loot

of earth-amber. For this, I am blamed—scapegoat,
who lent to woman a form of power. But it was you

who had a weakness for icon, put a standard to beauty.
I've eked a living from honing uncut matter into your

corsets of value. Truth is, there's no magic in glitter.
Spend an age in a sandbox, you'll know a stone for a stone.

Aluminum

Brilliant flickers in the ditches of a country road,
small suns stolen beneath dust-coated grasses.

The truck moves at the pace of a summer's day,
my father in the cab, Brian and I on the lowered tailgate.

We have to be careful of gold, those false gods—
bottle caps in sunlight, shattered glass, flecks

of mica—ornaments without worth of exchange.
My brother yells the signal, *aluminum*,

and the truck girds to a standstill. The two of us
hop down and gather discarded cans, slug-filled, each laid

careless as victims pulled from the aftermath of floods.
Seven cents for every pound, heaped in garbage bags

in the bed of the Chevy. What we were learning
was a way of living in the world—aware of what work

the earth under us would demand before it demanded us.
What we'd buy with the swag—speed bikes from the plant

where our father worked, seven dollars an hour,
*Hustler*s our friend Taylor sold on the schoolyard, a buck

for every rag. What we would own—the fortitude
of a sturdy shout. *Aluminum*, in love with a word

for the first time, the tongue's roll and caress of it,
something akin to windfall, spoils, the golden sour

fluids cataracting onto red clay—others' passions
grown cold in the night, puddling at our feet.

Turning Back

After leaving you, just miles out of Oklahoma the sky
was a thin ribbon of storm tied across a package of blue.

For months I considered how easy it would be.
I would gather my parcels of dust-bitten books,

albums of stilled memory and turn—not look back.
Then I slid atop the roadways doing just that—cruising

like a scud of clouds over grasslands,
sorghum licking the lengths of sky.

Around me, light faded as if it couldn't keep up the speed,
as from a shelter of coarse pine a coyote ran out—

the headlights sealing for an instant that golden look
of fear. It sounded so strange—the wheels

rolled over the thing, like hitting a bag of someone's
tossed-off laundry—a thin rattle of zipper or button,

a flannel sleeve seized round the axle.
I jerked the car over to the shoulder, peered

into the mirror at red eddies unfurling
in the vast Kansas distance. As I approached,

the thing heaved upon its side, back legs useless.
Not sure what to do, I came closer, bending instinctively,

to be driven back by a snarl and tight press of teeth.
We stared eye-to-eye—puddle-brown,

night-tinted green—till spaces tucked in around us.
I thought of how little there is of understanding,

how I have never been one to judge the frail
from the sound-hearted. The brute in me puffs

out its chest and pleads. *I love you. Let me go.*
I let it go, and as I pulled away I thought of you.

Not for the first time, but with the care of one touching
something newborn and soft—a gosling

or a cub's fistful of silver. It was then I looked back.
Quiet gathered round me like a crowd of strangers.

Flung into the darkness with the lot of Lot's wife—
of Orpheus and his tight-strung heart—

what we grasp is nothing in the end but what it means
to finish. You already know this—

what I saw is the road I've been through, disappearing,
in the night a few pinpoints of stars.

Devils 10 — Lucifer

Pick a card, any card. The jack of diamonds
has always been a favorite. I've found this city

suits me—Las Vegas, with its searing, lava
towers of light, the games of dice and domino.

My kind of people. Sit for an age or two
on a glacier, you'll learn to appreciate a fast ride,

neon strapped to buildings like threaded fire.
It was a gamble to come here, but what had I to lose?

The pale horse I bet on is a shoo-in, and you cry out
Swindle! Dirty pool! So sure you can see the strings

pulling together. My liaison with you has been,
shall we say, cursory. You were pawns on the board,

yet I marveled at the span of your hunger.
You have your moments. Who else would dare

a glittered city on such wastes as these? Your hope
is so unfounded. You come to the green felt, chancing

everything for a taste of larger life. I've found
fortune's threadbare garments suit me, but you

who'll lay blood on the dotted line, I've to salute—
headlong for abyss, bets placed on what's to catch you.

Eclipse

You remember the smell of paste, vivid flares
of construction paper, Mrs. King instructing you
which shapes to cut from what color. Now,
whenever you think *oval,* you'll think *pink*.

In kindergarten, lessons are made simple and primary.
You learn about life on the day of your first solar
eclipse, the light leaving you with a Styrofoam cup
of dirt, a handful of gritty seeds—marigolds.

Mrs. King directs you and your fellow classmates
to plant the granules deep in the earth you've contained.
Afterwards, you set them on a dark
windowsill, and as a boyish girl dares you to look

at the absence of the sky, you imagine pleated
heads blazing from the loam and silt. Bigger
than you, she grabs the back of your skull, forces
your gaze out the window. *Look at it,* someone instructs.

Now, whenever you think *circle* you'll think *black
with burning edges.* And the moment shortly after,
when your head is released and the circle goes white—
negative to positive. Your comrades will crowd

around you, peer into your dulled eyes and ask,
what did you see? You won't be able to answer,
having learned blindness is a state of mind
where no radiance enters and recognition begins.

Weeks later, marigolds will push their lion-heads
from under their crusts of soil—all but yours.
You'll take home your cup of unnourishing earth,
toss it in the bed of elephant ears beside the door.

Come next year, something bright will bend its way
around the shields of heart-shaped, green fronds.
This is another lesson you will learn. Loss can also
be gain. That though we be broken and sightless,

somewhere within us something springs from
a dense core, races toward the edges and the light.

Rhinestone

> *And what is an angel*
> *but a ghost in drag?*
> ~ Stan Rice, "Of Heaven"

Baron always hoped God would be a drag queen,
or so he told me the night I admitted I found no

comfort in things ecclesiastical. Both of us having
been born gay in the South, empty sockets in

the rhinestone buckle of the Bible Belt, we had
learned to cover our erections in church with hymn

books over our laps—a coy smile for Jesus in his
loincloth, hanging at the head of the pulpit. Baron,

brought up in an ascetic Baptist family, coped
by putting God in a wig, nine-inch heels that poked

through clouds as he walked. I imagine it made
the light less harsh, turned the cacophony of angels

into a magnificent floorshow. Saturday nights
at the bar under the interstate bridge, Baron rose

before the floor lamps—an evening star, glittered
and magenta. All night, he shaped the words

of other people's songs, brazenly tongued them.
In the beginning, only a word, then light enough.

Maybe it was as simple as *begin* or *open*. Perhaps,
it was heavier, like *fuck* or *cocksucker*—something

hot to start the air moving. All I've learned is silence
scares me secretly, for which I have Baron to thank.

Standing in a line of mourners filing their way
through the body of the church, Baron's mother

mourns before a backdrop of peace lilies and baby's
breath, her face a broken country of wet mascara rivers.

It was a closed-casket funeral, having lost an arm
on the way down the elevator shaft—it seemed appropriate

to everyone but me. I wanted to stand
before the congregation, give lip service to their psalms, say

I want you to know this. I need you to understand.
But words don't always change things. At least not for me.

Baron sauntered into my life wearing nothing
but chipped silver, pieces of light, twirling

to keep the dust off his body. He was nothing
if not movement. Baron's mother takes my hand

in hers, smiles weakly and gives the only mantra
she knows. *Jesus has taken him home.* I smile,

picturing Jesus in a Jackie O suit, wrap tied
at the nape of the neck, Adam's apple showing through.

Aubade

A day like this—

fields staggered with the movement
of choked weeds, hillsides of startled
purples, clusters of gold.

Consider the dull lulling of the cows,
unmovable in the rich muds of the radiant pond.
Consider the place where we stand,
on a railroad trestle burdened with blackbirds.

We see what these birds have seen.
The creek below us singing of what has
come before, and what goes after.

If you hold your breath, you can take it in—

not 'the bitter geography of loss,' its roads
cutting like wounds between dark passages of earth,
but the way light curves around everything,
draws the lowly into notice—the heavy-headed
weeds, brilliant ruins of slag.

And if you hold it a moment longer,
take the wind into your lungs,
it will send you on your way—
along those silvered tracks bent in the distance,

as if this were enough—
the two of us
seized against sky,
your scent housed in back of my throat.

Devils 11 —Void

Why must all absence be steeped in your terror?
Is it really so crushing to know there are no gilt

cities behind the curtains of heat? You were all
so like children—putting make-believe in the rose-

heads so winter could not touch them. How taxing
it must be to remember all the names of matter,

yet you fill star charts with a nomenclature
of the abstract, the immense unknown, antimatter.

What if it's all just noise? Flashes of light, shadows
in a cave? You say, *This is at least something!*

And you drape yourselves in the fleece of logic,
shudder under dim and distant galaxies. Yes, there's

a thing called the world. Everything that is.
Everything you boiled down to an essence and poured

into these conjunctions of symbol. Words! Even you
now discern their emptiness. You want to know

what I am. Not possible. For I am the lack between
name and the named, the silent pulse after being

decants. You'll feel better when there's nothing
to lay hands on. No fenced acre. No kingdom to come.

Tin

I. What the Queer Kid Was Thinking

When I was thirteen, my insides
looked like that rusted watering can in the backyard.
The one that made a life of collecting rain,

grafting whale-skin algae along its sides.
You could see the ripple of mosquito larvae
thread the water like thin scribbles of birds

children place in the skylines of their pictures.
I pretended I could keep my soul in that can,
out of reach, wrapped in riverweed.

There it would gather seasons—sudden
downpours of summer, thin membranes of ice in November—
dug down in dark, golden silt along the base.

We all grow in puddles, halfway between vapor and dirt,
vital as any child's want of dark corners. I stole
safety under pleats of surface-muck,

found cold truth in scum and wet cinders, the shiver
of names schoolboys threw in my face. I never
fit loosely into my skin, and when you're stretched

tight enough anyone can see scripture written on your bones.
I had to be a Freudian slip in God's vocabulary.
He'd meant to say *gleaming*. He'd meant to say *silver*.

Only it hadn't come out quite right—energy dissipated
under the surface, in the dimness of the pool's center.
He'd meant to say *goldfish with whiskers, lotuses blossoming pink*.

He'd wanted clay, not cracked-lip earth under ultraviolet.
Maybe I grew tired of awaiting answers to prayers.
What's more, my skinned knees could've been better used

at other altars. I only wanted someone to say
pagan, and really mean it—whisper *abomination*
so I would know this was a word for any creature

who could change its shape, devolve
to a silver mosquito for the boys' tight bodies—
piercing and pulling their insides out.

II. If I Only Had a Heart

Stand perfectly still, and the world won't notice.
On the walls of my grandmother's home is a family
frozen under sheets of flaring glass—arrested smiles,

stiff joints. In the country, dirt is everywhere.
My mother tells us not to move, not to stain anything
as we smile for the camera. It's my grandparents'

fiftieth wedding anniversary, and the family
looks as if they could be stood upon cakes.
The photographer, in a pink Oxford, directs

us where to stand. Husbands and wives together,
youth seated at their feet. In bursts of light,
we are taken in and held forever, ghosts surfacing

from a chemical wash. Later, unnoticed, I hear
uncles joke about the photographer. *How do queers
fake orgasms,* they ask. *They spit on your back.*

I wanted to be a burning catalyst then, to set things
in motion, but somehow I got stuck in the amber.
Years after, I let my first boyfriend fuck me

in a broken field, scent of opened earth under us,
just to see how soiled I could get.
Then it seemed like the whole world had me

naked and on the run. My Uncle Jim pulled
me aside at a family gathering to say he was sorry
for anything said in ignorance. Around us,

oblivious cousins cartwheeled through clover,
brothers sent Nerf footballs in crescents through
the air. They asked me to join them. Silence was

always hardest to suffer. The way we close ourselves
behind gloss. There are reasons why worlds
are kept in motion. If you stand still long enough,

rust encircles the heart. Do you know about
oil, lubrication? Have you heard about forgiveness?

Silver

As with everything, there is a need for a beginning.
Catalysts of rainwater and earth-mulch, influences of tide
fetch silver-bellied frogs to the muddy lips of ponds,
their skins an oil slick of poisons, the savor of bitter loam.

They make of their lives something barely decipherable—
undersides of leaves, gray-lichened robes of the trees.
Each are diminished at the swampy margins,
mislaid to view, acknowledged only by their voices.

Yet you do not doubt their attendance in the congress
of the field. They are the reedy ideas of song.
Consider what this means, the loss of oneself to ambient
camouflage, your homeland any soft element of earth.

NOTES

"Devils 1 – Beelzebub":

The name literally means "lord of flies." The gospel version of Beelzebub originated from the fly-god of the Phoenicians, Ahriman, who entered the world in the form of a fly.

"a book and a bell": Reading from the Bible and the ringing of bells (specifically church bells) were the two principle charms used to dispel the Devil.

"Devils 2 – Mephistopheles":

Mephistopheles was the name given to the devil in Goethe's *Faust*.

> *czardas*: 1. An intricate Hungarian dance characterized by variations in tempo. 2. Music for this dance.

"Devils 3 – Coyote":

Coyote is the vulgar but sacred trickster figure in many Native American oral traditions. Among other things, he is said to have stolen fire from the Fire Beings and hidden it in Wood.

"Devils 4 – Grendel":

The monster Beowulf conquers in the Teutonic epic.

In Old English, "monster" referred to a divine omen, indicating misfortune; akin of "monstrare" to show, point out, indicate, and "monere" to warn.

"Iron":

Lines 25 and 26 in italics are taken from W. H. Auden's poem "The Witnesses."

"Devils 5 – Cobra":

The practice of snake charming in India has largely been outlawed due to the charmers' inhuman treatment of the cobras. Many charmers were known to sew up the mouths of their snakes with black thread, thereby preventing them from striking.

"Devils 6 – Pan":

Plutarch wrote that a sailor named Thamus, while passing the Echinades Island in the region of Tiberius, heard a voice cry out: "The great god Pan is dead."

The Christian Devil inherited his cloven hooves, exaggerated phallus, and horns from the god, Pan.

"Seagulls at the Local Walmart in a Landlocked State":

The form of this poem was inspired by the *National Audubon Society Field Guide to North American Birds*.

"Devils 7 – Lilith":

In Hebrew mythology, Lilith was the first wife of Adam, who was replaced by Eve due to Lilith's headstrong insistence that she was Adam's equal. As punishment, she was thrown from the Garden and cursed by the Lord to never be able to bear human children. However, she is said to have later coupled with demons and given birth to the succubi.

"Sherrie's Poem":

Lines in italics are taken from Pablo Neruda's *Cien sonetos de amor XI & C*.

"Devils 8 – Marduk":

God of the Spring Sun. Marduk was originally an Assyro-Babylonian vegetation god. In Sumerian myth, he and the goddess Aru fashioned "the seed of mankind."

Over time, the aspect of Marduk became more terrible. Brass images of him were erected in his temples. Their bellies opened down the center like a pair of gates, and within these idols a furnace burned. Into these fires, the priests of Marduk threw countless sacrifices.

"Devils 9 – Azazel":

In Leviticus, Yahweh instructs Aaron to take goats and draw lots for them. He is instructed to "allot one to Yahweh and the other to Azazel" in the desert (Lev. 16:8-10). The goat sent into the wilderness was said to carry the sins of the tribe with it. This is where the term "scapegoat" originates.

In Jewish mythology, it is Azazel who shows women how to use cosmetics and jewelry to attract men.

"Aubade":

"the bitter geography of loss" is a reference to Ezra Pound's cautions on the image, published in *Poetry* in 1913.

ACKNOWLEDGMENTS

I am grateful to the editors of the following publications in which a number of these poems (some in earlier versions) first appeared:

Aux Arc Review: "Turning Back"
Barrelhouse: "Bees" and "Canada Geese on the Lawn of Frasier Meadows Retirement Community"
California Quarterly: "Devils 1 — Beelzebub"
Chariton Review: "Seagulls at the Local Walmart in a Landlocked State"
Comstock Review: "Devils 9 — Azazel" as "Devil"
Crab Creek Review: "Devils 5 — Cobra"
Crab Orchard Review: "Silver," "Eclipse" as "Fire," "Devils 4 — Grendel," and "Devils 10—Lucifer"
Cream City Review: "Sherrie's Poem"
Hawai'i Pacific Review: "Tin" as "What the Queer Kid Was Thinking"
Hayden's Ferry Review: "Arabesque"
The Lucid Stone: "Static"
Minnesota Review: "Devils 7 — Lilith"
New Millennium Writings: "Chlorine" and "Losing the Thread" as "Iodine: A Love Poem"
North American Review: "Nickel," "Rhinestone," and "Devils 3 — Coyote"
Now and Then: The Appalachian Magazine: "Milkweed"
Pinyon: "Aluminum"
Poet Lore: "Aubade" as "Oxygen"
Spoon River Poetry Review: "Iron"
Square One: "Metallurgy," "Letter Found in Abandoned Backpack — Mosquito Lake, Alaska" as "Magic," "Silicone," and "Devils 8 — Marduk"
Wascana Review: "Piss Yellow"

"Silicone" was also included in *Low Explosions: Writings on the Body* (Knoxville Writers' Guild, 2006); "Tin" in an alternate version titled "What the Queer Kid Was Thinking" was reprinted in *Hawai'i Pacific Review: Best of the Decade 1997–2007* (vol. 21, 2007).

I am deeply indebted to Lorna Dee Cervantes, Marcia Douglas, Jeffrey Robinson, Marilyn Kallet, Arthur Smith, Steve Sparks, Ashley van Doorn, Kristi Maxwell, Matt Gilchrist, Stanton Garner, Allen Dunn, Charlotte Pence, and the Knoxville Writers' Guild for their support, encouragement, editorial advice, and general warm spirits. A special thanks as well to Jay Parini for taking a chance on this manuscript.

About the Author

Bradford Tice, a native of Tennessee, received his MA in English from the University of Colorado and his Ph.D. from the University of Tennessee. In 2009 he began teaching writing and literature at Nebraska Wesleyan University. Both a poet and fiction writer by trade, his work has appeared in such periodicals as *The Atlantic Monthly*, *North American Review*, *The American Scholar*, *One Story*, *Epoch*, as well as in *Best American Short Stories 2008*. Tice is also the recipient of numerous Pushcart nominations and was named the winner of the Prairie Schooner 2009 Edward Stanley Award for poetry. He lives in Lincoln, Nebraska, with his partner Christopher Lynch.

Tice won New Rivers Press' Many Voices Project prize for poetry in 2011 with his manuscript for *Rare Earth*, selected from a highly competitive field by finalist judge Jay Parini.